AF654729

Be the

light

Copyright © 2026 Sayina Nila

Published by Cogitabund LLP, India
publishing@cogitabund.com
www.cogitabund.com

BE THE LIGHT

A Cogitabund Book/ published by arrangement with the author

The characters and events portrayed in this book are fictitious. Any similarity to real persons, living or dead, is coincidental and not intended by the author

No part of this book may be reproduced, stored in a retrieval system, or transmitted in any form or by any means, electronic, mechanical, photocopying, recording, or otherwise, without express written permission of the publisher

ISBN: 978-93-49383-41-8

Typeset and Cover Design by Cogitabund LLP

Contents

Be the Light

Sayina Nila

Thanks to the Almighty.
This book is dedicated to my beloved parents.

IQRA

Recites from your heart,
It resonates with the soul.
Read and read, you will find
that everything holds a purpose.
Everyone has a calling from beyond!
Read not just the ink, but the shades of sky,
the heartbeat of cosmos, the patience of Earth,
the kindness folded in nightfall.
Read the hope embraced in every dawn!
Read the spoken silence and
the unspoken words!
Read your wounds; they are the lessons.
Read your tears, they are the shadowed prayers.
Read within the lines of life…
and write your own!

A BEGINNING BLOOMED...

A prayer is listened to,
before it rose from the heart.
The journeys are already destined,
the pain
and the love
born before it cherished.
The seeds of my soul,
dreamed before myself.
I am on the way,
by just holding the hope
to be grateful.

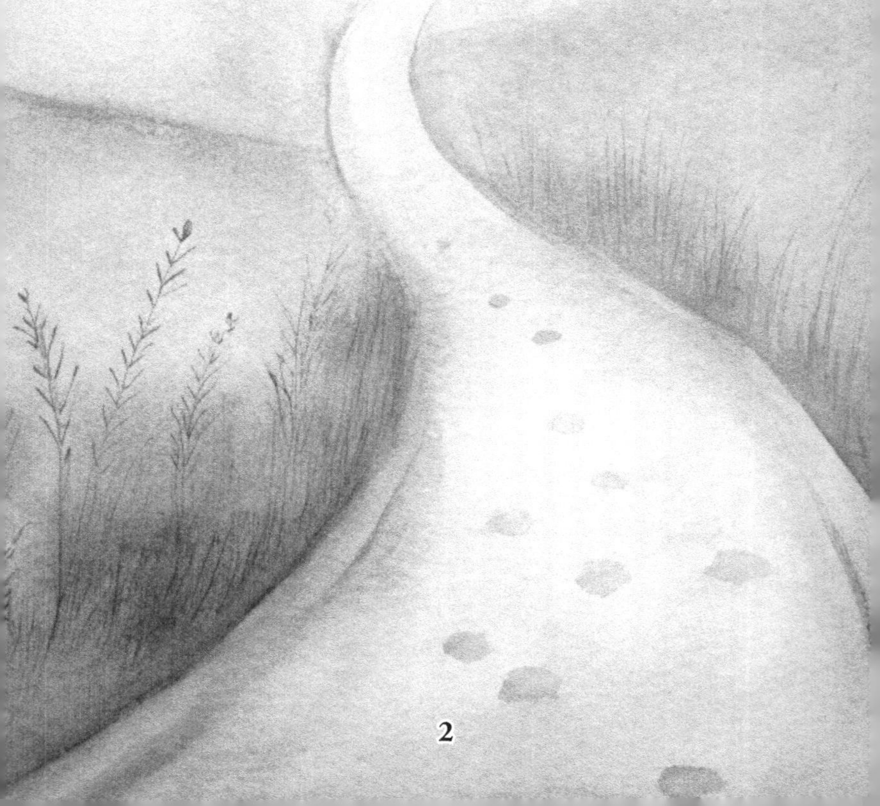

HOME…

I am in the arms of peace.
By the shades of love…
I am just making art.
With the broken pieces of my heart.
Here, I am free from myself!
I love to be real, and
I am healing here.
Cheers to the fears,
Let's have this cup of time together.

LET YOUR SMILE SHINE

The energetic smiles of the sky,
Fallen on our dreams.
Catch it, hold on to the truth.
Kiss it by your soul; then.
Send it to the universe through
The ship of hope.
By the taken promise and the spoken silence,
Can we break the darkness?
Can we go beyond the light year?
there our souls united, in the
realm of eternity.
Yes, my beloved,
Spread love,
Enlighten the smiles,
You are the starlit!

THE LOVE

The feather of my soul
fell into the orbit of your heart,
The time revolves around us.
The skyline of our dreams;
meets frequently,
and it seeks
for the harmony.
I leave you in the
Streets of our desires.
From there and here,
You follow forever!
Eternally, you become my home,
And then I am another you!

BEYOND THE HORIZON

Without knowing each other,
How will you know the
depth of the deep love?
How will you hug highly?
By the embraced roots of hearts?
The words that crossed
over the silence, are not worthy.
Then, why are we talking too much?
What is the finite
between you and me,
Like it evolved from a single drop?
We are just you and me, right?
Then, where can we discover 'us'?
First, fix yourself,
Then we can seek each other.
Then we can fly...
by holding our wings together,
into the endless dream!
There, we can compose
the beats of silence
by the beads of love.

RAIN IN THE DESERT

In the desert of dreams,
The same waves
hits on the
shores of the heart,
again and again,
time dissolves,
love evolves,
tears dry up, and
The hope preserved.
But again, and again
It hugs the soul
and enlighten the way!

THE SHIP IN THE SKY!

I am floating
in the flow of time.
To and fro,
In the depth of my love.
Up and down,
in every part of my dreams.
The compass in the heart,
led me so far:
and still long way to go.
It is a well-planned journey,
And I am just tracing.
my destined story;
to reveal the untold purpose and,
Then, to give a cheer to myself.

Like the sky,
the boundless hope
set me in this deep blue.
Beyond the horizons,
I want to fly deeply.

MIRAGE OF SILENCE

You came to me,
in between the shades of
Reality and destiny.
In this desert of silence,
I am singing the rhythm of serenity.
to myself.
At the right time,
our seeds of hope will bloom!
We will fly in the blue sky.
We will fly, my friend!

THE GRAVITY OF LIFE

Life is twinkling.
Between the promises
unforgivable desires to be alive, and
to live in the moment.
But the existence,
A wave in the middle of
final time and destined future.

Going deeper and deeper
Into the curls of the heart,
and to the roots of the presence,
thereby sticking out to the highs.

I found my dreams.
They are pondering in the dark.
I think the thoughts are
The twilight to spark the dawn of reality.
Spin me into you, like a black hole.
Hug me with your lyric,
Like the silence rebound
from the rhythm of fullness.

Read the epic of time,
from the eyes decode my soul,
in between the breath,
that we have shared.
Beyond the time and space.
We can dive into love and explore.

REASONS OF HEART!

It's hard; hold yourself.
It's broken; let the light get in.
It's challenging; embrace it with the hope of love.
Beyond the seasons of time,
Hold the reasons of heart…
to enlighten the life.
Just listen to your heart and keep going!

THE SYLLABLES OF HEART!

All the time,
So compassionate to recite love!
But, in this chancy life,
in-between the chaos,
learn to be silent.
Storms of life taught that,
Not everyone deserves
the warmth of the pure heart.
Being the cornerstone,
ignored and rejected
Then I built the empire.
with the syllables of love, peace, and empathy
for welcoming the true ones.
Being in the middle of the story,
Choosing peace over anything,
and dissolving into the realm of eternity.
Paved my own way to wisdom
Cherishing the little things with huge gratitude,
Being the bridge
holding each other all the time
to imprint the prints of my soul,
heartfully in this beautiful world.

STAINS OF SILENCE

Darkness sparkles the light,
where I am cradled by air.
I filled my scattered thoughts.
with stars, and
weaved my strains by stains of silence:
then into the spring of my dreams.

KISMET

Retracing the dispersed
breath..,and
trying and trying to
connect the dots,
It ends at the dole.
The heart out hope,
The sprint in the dark
lightens the way.
The beloved solitary
dip in the smile.
To connect the dots
and finish the secret circle,
Life needs me.
Without knowing the game,
Scattered life
fizzle out the destined love,
to behold my existence.

SEASONS OF THE JOURNEY

When your world
breaks into pieces,
Be your own peace!

The pain... paints the heart,
With the true colors.
The rain in the desert,
twinkling tears,
makes the rainbow.
The storms make the
waves of calm.
All demands,
The reasons for the purity.
No need to explain, be silent.

In the struggles,look into yourself.
Warm your soul with prayers.
burn like the sun, and just be your own light.

Throughout the
seasons of this journey,
All you have is yourself!
Whatever it is,
Go on with yourself.
Hold your hope and light all the way..!

THE LOST WAY

The lost way led me to the stars of my sky!
It's all about the choices.
And the pieces of love
determines the destiny of the soul.
How to retrace the time,
To get a better plan
For the broken heart
And the faded dreams?
Tell me, where can we plant?
this tree of hope?

LOST AND FOUND

Until the end of this voyage,
holding the roots of my soul,
evolving into the plants of destiny,
blooming beyond the barriers
wrapped with the tears of joy
and defined my dream.
Slowly the story
disappears in between the beats of the heart,
Lost, found, and guided again!
Come on, let's paint this life.
With the everlasting colors of love
And then we can return to the realm of unity.

BE YOU

Each flower has a story.
of tolerance, curled with its own petals.
Have patience;
You will own
The gain for your pain!
The soul starts to bloom;
be here now,
be calm,
Be kind and be you.

COCOON

Like the buried seed,
I am longing for the spring.
Through the seasons of my heart,
The falling leaves of my dreams.
Raise the strength deep within.
It is so smarting,
so propel to the edge of my existence.
For the shades of the truth,
flowering of love…
to being myself
and for my calling!
With the beats of sabr,
Within the cocoon of time,
I am spinning my wings for the sky!

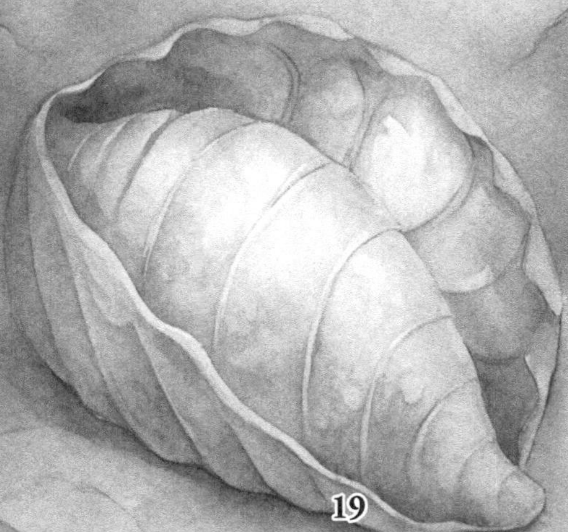

GRATEFUL ALWAYS…

I don't take things for granted.
I feel soulful….,
For the smell of soil, when it
kissed by the rain.
I become hopeful.
for the flap of a butterfly.
I feel loved when I watch the twinkling stars.
In this very way,
I am grateful for all the trances of my life;
for the here and now,
for my little space in this universe,
the hidden tears,
the silent smiles,
broken heart and the little wins
unwavering love all along my paths,
and for all the truly inspired little things!

SANCTUARY OF SELF!

Beyond all the way,
All through the stars
Is there a way
Back to me?
Is there a way back to my roots?
Is there a way back to my love?
Is there a way back to my dreams?
I am unfolding myself to find myself again,
to restart again with more courage!

KINTSUGI

I collect myself
From the scattered
pieces of my soul,
in the light of hope.
Losing in the midst of chaos;
and healing in the depth of love.
Life has to go on…
To search the roots of my existence,
and to delight in the truth!
I am learning who I am again,
I am piecing myself together.
With a touch of compassion.
The scars are the stories,
Imperfections shine,
when viewed with the heart.
I am my own Kintsugi-
Broken
Mended and
Graceful.

RISE AGAIN

At some point in life,
Truth resonates:
We fell deeply into the reality,
where continuing becomes more struggling
than concluding.
It's okay, you may breathe now.
This too shall pass, and let it be!
Rise again....,
Let hope be your light,
Let you be free from fears.
and led by the heart.

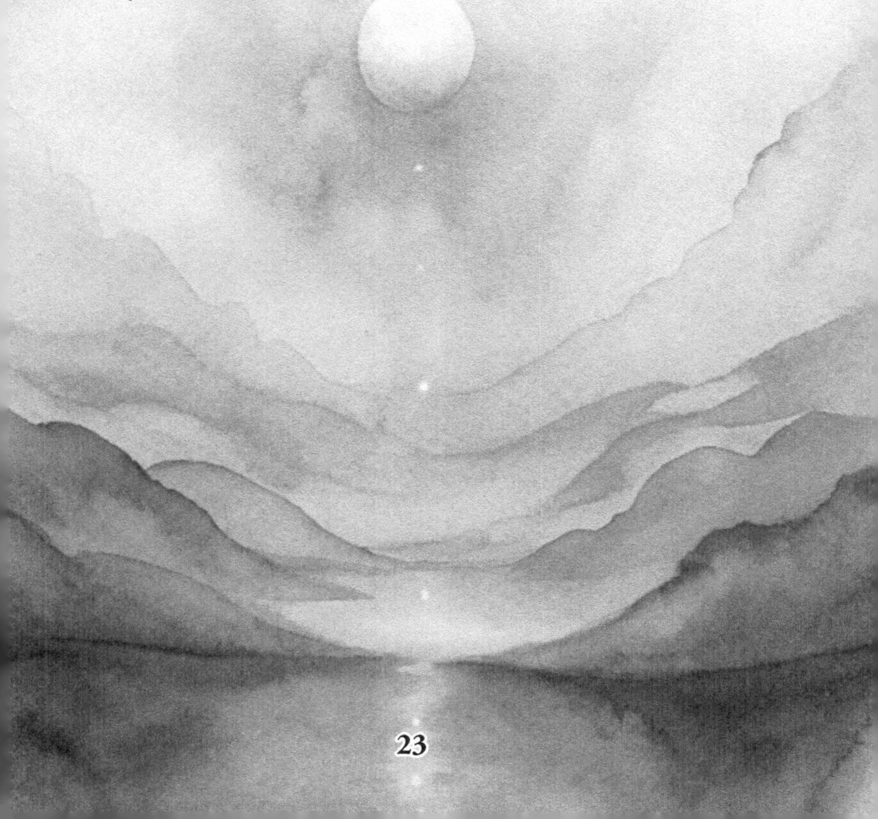

MAKTUB

The fallen leaves..,
are messages from beyond
and they are telling that;
Nothing lasts forever
Everything happens for a reason.
All along the way,
Life teaches what words cannot say,
Wounds may whisper, yet hearts will mend.
Hope will rise.
Guided by the Eternal
every step lights up the skies,
leading us to the everlasting serenity.

TIME AND TIDE

Beside the seaside,
I sip the stillness.
Time and tide.
Heals the way to myself.
When I searched
The unwavering dreams;
The world inside the shells
Whispered to embrace the unknown!
Stars gazed at the seashore.
and it warmly enlightens my heart,
woven with the unlearned letters of love.
Again, life blooms beautifully.
In deep and beyond the horizons.

COUNT YOUR BLESSINGS!

It is always something.
Behind our hearts and
Beyond our hands.
Believe it, there is a purpose.
For this delightful journey!
Trust the process, enjoy it fully.
Each moment longing
for deep love and peace.
Traverse the raindrops of your ocean, be the flow.
You are a shore of precious stones,
and just start building your own empire!
Lighten the joy of togetherness,
Count your blessings!
Keep going…..
Keep growing.

RADIANT LIGHT WITHIN

The dark hit the soul,
Then into the lit.
Deep silence into the
Harmony of heart,
Off the beaten path and
the knock-back; are just
Interventions from beyond!
I dipped my soul
Here and there;
Beholden myself.
Lost and lost again,
Seeking solace, and I found it.
The sun awakens the moonlight, and it.
lulled the darkness.
Stars just arise from seeds of eternity,
The dark and dawn sing hope.
At last, every day
Life transcends boundaries;
Fading to flourish..,
Remove to Renew.
Like a lantern in the dark,
The inner light illuminates paths unseen,
Life turns into a more radiant you!

BE THE FLOW

In letting go,
let your heart glide.
In every wave,
let your soul reside.
Be the river
Be the rain
flow through joy
flow through pain
hand in hand
dive into life.

THE GLOBAL EMPATHY

The tree within the seed whispers softly:
"Plant hope deep in your soul.
The heart nourishes it with gentle love.
And prayers hold it with compassion.
It grows into the world of humanity,
Flourishing in shades of shared empathy.
Hand in hand,
Heart to heart,
Life to life,
From one to all,
Dreams rise together.
Smiles blossoms.
Joy shared.
Peace flows freely, touching every soul."

BE THE LIGHT…

Oh, my soul friend,
This is for you.
You are the blessing,
Throughout the seasons of my life.
You are the silver linings of my soul forever.
Dear ray of hope,
Do miracles
By love and passion.
Behold the light;
Believe in your heart, it will show the way.
I want to fill my world.
with the joy of your success,
and your goodness.
Make your own story.
fill it with compassion,
You can do it, my charm!
Be the light….!

9 789349 383418

Printed at Repro India Ltd.